COURAGE AT THREE AM

A.W. Richard Sipe

 Friesenpress

Suite 300 - 990 Fort St
Victoria, BC, Canada, V8V 3K2
www.friesenpress.com

ISBN
978-1-5255-1039-7 (Hardcover)
978-1-5255-1040-3 (Paperback)
978-1-5255-1041-0 (eBook)

1. Poetry, Subjects & Themes, Inspirational & Religious

Distributed to the trade by The Ingram Book Company

CONTENTS

BOOKS BY A.W. RICHARD SIPE

Hope, Psychiatry's Commitment
Editor 1970

A Physician in the General Practice of Psychiatry
Selected Papers of Leo H. Bartemeier
Editor with Peter Martin & Gene Usdin 1970

Beyond Crescent Gate
Fifteen Poems of Dr. Walter Jahrreiss
Editor 1970

Psychiatry, Ministry & Pastoral Counseling
Editor with Clarence J. Rowe 1984

A Secret World: Sexuality and the Search for Celibacy
1990

Sex, Priests and Power: The Anatomy of a Crisis
1996

Celibacy: A Way of Loving, Living and Serving
1996

Celibacy In Crisis
2003

Living the Celibate Life: A Search for Models and Meaning
2004

Sex, Priests, and Secret Codes: The Catholic Church's
2000 Year Paper Trail of Sexual Abuse
with Thomas Doyle & Patrick Wall 2006

The Serpent and the Dove: Celibacy in Literature and life
2007

I Confess: How a Very Religious Catholic Boy Learned Dirty Words Sex
and Celibacy Avoided Suicide Embraced Death Found Love God & Himself
Not Necessarily in That Order
2016

In his new book of poems, *Courage at Three AM*, Richard Sipe continues the reckoning he began in *I Confess* – but with a difference. These new poems are more personal and unguarded, closer to the bone. Sipe grapples with the discouragement and the terror of old age, and the weariness that comes from fighting a powerful institution. He began his work on the inside, as a therapist helping his fellow priests. But over the years, his scholarship on celibacy and his advocacy for the survivors of clergy abuse brought him more and more into conflict with the church that had been his spiritual home. In a remarkable long poem in the new collection, reminiscent of James Merrill's Ouija-board books, Sipe imagines an encounter with Judas that ultimately resolves that conflict – he feels an affinity for the man another poet has called "Saint Judas."

Ultimately Sipe finds a solution to the despair of old disagreements and old age in the youthful sources of his commitment – a beautiful poem evokes his vivid boyhood memory of a Minnesota morning. Other poems imagine his experience back to infancy, the core of Catholic imagery. And in a poem about death, Sipe parses all the time of his life down to the present infinitesimal moment, a happy counterpart to the anguished, early morning moment of the book's title. These poems are by turns mystical and practical – in the end, Sipe takes simple comfort in the example of abuse survivors and in his friends. This is a book about time, and its most enduring image is of a first visit with a friend, the "instant of enthrall" when the "years of disclosure" began.

Terence McKiernan, President

BishopAccountability.org

FOREWORD

Years ago, Richard Sipe opened his door to me on a sunny day in La Jolla, California. I had spied a flickering humming bird as I walked from my car to his gate and taken it to be a wonderful omen. It was. In addition to opening his door, Richard opened his heart and poured out all that he felt and knew about matters of hope, loss, faith, disillusion, love and anger. In other words, he taught me of the human condition.

Lucky for us, Richard has continued to look within and without to find what is true and to give generously of what he discerns. In these poems, we find a warrior who is unafraid of tangling with the most difficult challenge of life, including its end.

"Tell no lies / As you give me to my grave" writes Richard, and I know that he means it, for this is a man who tells the truth about himself so that we may know ourselves better. The consolation we have knowing that he, and we, will pass includes this great book of poems.

Savor it.

MICHAEL D'ANTONIO
Pulitzer Prize Winning Investigative Journalist

DEDICATION

Andrew Karim Kader, MD, PhD
Courageous and kind physician

PREFACE

The importance of courage—its indispensability—for a life well lived needs no defense. I have found that my life and loves depend on this fulcrum. Courage may seem incidental, exhibited in a moment of heroism, but I am convinced that it is a facet of daily life and character.

The foundations of courage are laid down in the first and ongoing struggles for existence. Some of my reflections take me to the child's crib. My personal history has propelled me from the crib to the cloister and to the service of the suffering—those who have had to fight courageously because of challenges from neglect or abuse.

Yes, I discovered, like so many others, my trek has been guided by my friend, Courage.

A prior book of poems, *I CONFESS*, developed from an unintentional creative concomitant to a psychotherapeutic endeavor of self-confrontation. It turned out to be a memoir. Who knew, least of all me, it would flow into a poetic tradition pioneered by Walt Whitman? This series completes my venture into self-examination and poetry and continues an incidental memoir. I found that survival flourished as I embraced my humanity.

My initial reflections bubbled across the pebbles and streams of a moderately chaotic small-town Catholic boy and family—what could be passed off as ordinary traumatic incidents. But even ordinary trauma comingles with the darker questions of life, love and struggles for relationships, meanings and existence.

This series of reflections also bores into one subterranean territory of trauma—the all-too-common abuse of minors and the vulnerable.

Trauma has been an area of focus of my life work, especially sexual betrayal by the trusted—mainly Roman Catholic clergy. Never a clergy victim myself, I learned compassion and empathy from advocacy, associations with courageous men and women and a nature tilted toward the sensitive.

How does one endure the discovery, exposure, advocacy, for victims and confrontation with religions generating, protecting and denying atrocities they continue to foster and permit?

I hope this question-alert does not present the reader with a too-morose, off-putting invitation. In the end, I hope these thoughts and images encourage those who have suffered trauma so they know they are not alone. There is hope. That is one reward of courage.

The last reflections in this collection expose my training as a theologian, a fact I have never tried to disguise. But neither have I imposed on any religion's faith. Two fundamental organizing principals of my thinking are represented by these expressions: the unity of realities, human-transient / eternal-divine, and the life drive to fulfil our humanity—to become human in the fullness of that meaning.

All aspects of life, art, literature, religion and science have to do with being human—life has "consilience," in E. O. Wilson's meaning of unity. Any divine plan has more to do with this reality than suffering and death that has been severely distorted (spiritualized i.e. martyrdom) in religious tradition and practice. Religion is for living. The personal—and universal—life and death, and thoughts about the incarnational and Judas narratives, will be self-evident as I struggle with realities about human trauma.

In this collection, mine is an appeal for hope—psychiatrists' and all healers' commitment. My appeal to hope is the "rage, rage, rage" that Dylan Thomas counsels the aging person faced with death; the determination to live and carry on the fight.

From where comes the courage to keep up the fight? Where is the rage to stay loyal to the ideals of one's youth and discover new things? This is the struggle I live in these outpourings.

There are joys and pains that we should never forget—the courage to remember infuses vitality, and opens ever-new vistas and wonders. Some of these thoughts and feelings can only be approached and processed at three A.M.

AWRS

mmorgenstern

PROLOGUE

THREE A.M.

Henry David Thoreau cites Napoleon Bonaparte for considering "The three-o'-clock-in-the-morning courage"— *the rarest*—even compared to soldiering in the front lines of battle.

There is a lore about three a.m.: a time when one is alone, without support, companionship or counsel—on one's own, lonely, even bereft of comfort.

Joni Mayhan describes the phenomenon: *"As the clock approaches the hour of 3AM, something strange happens in the world around us. The veil between the living and the dead grows thinner, allowing free passage between the two dimensions. Demons, ghosts and inter-dimensional creatures slip into the land of the living, creating havoc and tormenting us as we lay in bed sleeping. They call it the Devil's Hour"*

WARRIOR'S LAMENT

I

The evanescent mist of dawn
shimmers over now-green field of strife.
Clouds float, billow above
casting shadows fleeting gloom,
ghostly warriors, conflict consumed.

Sun-shafts pierce the air like missiles
to obliterate a battalion or soldiers one by one.
The dappled field presages splotches
reserved for blood and night.
The enemy will not be silent
much past pink morning light.

There comes a time when a warrior
needs to hang his shield
and fall upon his sword.
Is this my moment?
When shield glows in morning's rays
my bloodied sword still boasts some victory.
Or should I wait till dusk?
Dark shadows forming cover enough.
When dismembered youth besmirch the trodden turf
wounds ooze red blood and yellow pus;
stink of sweat and death gobbles up the air.
Bets placed and cashed. The race is done.
The haze of hate—mortal struggle—strangles
atmosphere and stifles breath.

What will it take to skirmish one more day?
What maiden's kerchief will emblaze my heart?
How to conjure Galahad's strength of ten?

II

The foe, formidable, is fearsome.
What chance against such power?
Hate that cloaks itself in righteousness.

Ravages of war register
in dents upon my saving shield.
Blows inflicted mark my trusted sword.
I relinquish a sacred shield with reverence
having served a friend well.
I review the scars of conflict—
healing red orange wounds,
purple blue bruises between fresh gashes
oozing green and yellow pus.

Death blow, price of interminable war,
so far has me eluded.
Shall I beat death at its game?
My sword tip
directed straight above my heart.
No rib diverts its mission.

III

The scabs of mind and heart rebel.
They moan,
"the cause, the cause, the cause,
not you, the cause.
You serve at life's discretion."

Love does not cringe at death,
nor count of the battle cost.
Cause abandoned
is loss of self and meaning.
Courage is just hanging on.

BABY CRIES

I cry. I have no words
to say it hurts.

I cry in dark.
I feel scared.

I cry; I am alone,
not knowing lonely word.

My tummy empty.
Deep, deep, empty.

No food will fill it.
All I can do is cry.

Cry of hope that you will know
what my tears are spelling,

asking, demanding; anger without bound,
frustration, my tone, terror, tantrum.

Yes, wounded child
you carry heavy burden.

Early scars penetrate deepest
to the core, distort, torment.

Not for a moment,
but a million moments.

These are the battles
fought at three in night.

Tears cleanse, courage tested,
victory sealed in the dark of fright.

Your heart is bursting.
Born just, does fate follow this soon?

I cry. I trust you.
Help me as you dry my tears.

mmorgenstern

SOMEDAY

Someday

I'll have words
to tell you how I feel
in this crib.

I see, I think, I learn.
When you hold me, give me warm milk,
contentment envelops me
from head to toe.

You give life; you pick me up
and let me touch your cheek
pull your ear, pinch your nose
and poke your eye.

When I can't see or you disappear,
everything ends. I don't know time; only now.
When you come back, the now
springs alive again—so do I.

You dry so many tears—comfort me in dark
hold me close, calm my fears
yet miss a reservoir of tears
unseen.

Emptiness comes and goes, casts an infernal shadow.
Even now I search for strength to dissolve
the mist of living now
and someday outside this cage.

websipe

TELL ME ONE MORE TIME

Tell me one more time you love me
as you tuck me in to sleep.

Just because I cannot talk yet
doesn't mean I don't understand.

You say things in gibberish
too big for me right now,

but I know your tone.
I read your face, your smile.

You read me too.
My heart thumps tuned to your smile,

your laugh. Some indefinable
silliness—a moment promising life.

I can read your face without sound—
I love you, written plain

in a moment,
takes away the pain.

And now I can sleep
in peace.

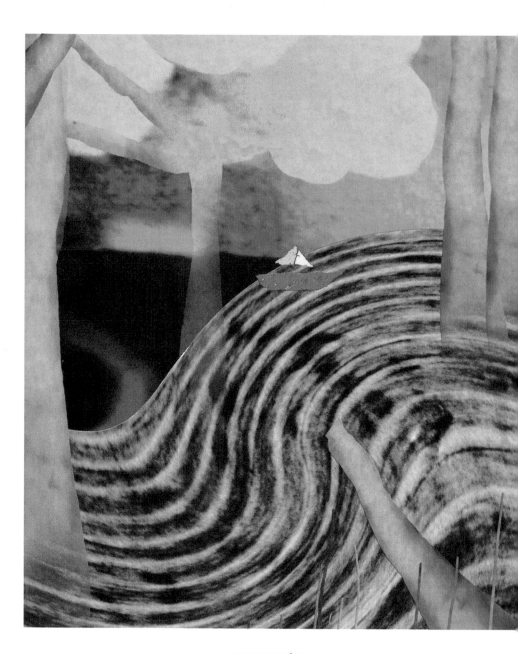

mmorgenstern

MINNESOTA MORNING

For Marcelo

Dew-drenched, new-mown grass
beneath my running feet,

intoxicating fragrance clean.
My heels hit the still-cool concrete walk

and strike the soft warm tarmac.
Untrimmed sedges line the highway.

Timothy, June and manna grass
prick my ankles, toes. No detour, slow not either.

The granite chips along the tracks
quicken my step. I dance lightly to their sharper tune.

The smooth silk steel rail soothes whatever pain
the trek has cost my soles so far.

II

I lay in the shade of the cottonwood tree, look up.
The breeze plays tender tambourine with leaves and pods.

Cotton floats like snow,
proclaiming his generative promise in gentle puffs.

Strong, tolerant of storm and floods,
tears endured and friendship found.

I breathe freedom in its soothing shade,
open to the clouds and sky—my province.

Hear the meadowlark in the long grass
heralding hope for unfettered flight.

III

The pearl-sandy road leads two blocks to the lake.
Soft surface takes my prints with comfort warmth.

The beach oozes green between my toes.
Relaxed-blue ribbons lure me deeper, baptize
my naked-dusted body-soul.

Intimacy between natures flourishes
on the prairies that fight back summer
fire and glow golden in the fall.

A mission found—
To be free, to be me.

Follow, young man, your heart's path;
the morning of youth is fleeting,

but everywhere is Minnesota
in the morning.

PEGASO
PARA MATEO

My wing-ed friend
with angels' breath and form,
lightning grace, mystical movement,
whose trot or touch on earth
springs springs that flow
and cleanse,
your bifurcated being knew my heart,
gave me voice and vision.

Pegasus, my muse,
your red-grey-blue-white wings
bedazzle and mesmerize
give flight to my soul
unleash me from my earthly bonds
transport me, if not to stars,
at least to the gates of *Paradiso*
with Dante and his muse
where love is unbounded,
unfettered and free.

Pegasus, my Pegasus,
I ride you not with bit and bridle
nor dare like arrogant Bellerophon to tame you.

You guide the direction of my destiny.

Your genesis from blood and foam,
so different from my own;
mortality divergent in our spheres
but not unlike in strife, striving, struggles, fears.

Wing-ed being of heaven and earth
fashioned creature, fabricated and
fated to contradict, in conflict, like me birth-ed.

Your immortality already locked in heaven.
What of the stars infuses our poor dust?

Mine in flux, tethered to crafted words
but winging toward a loving heart or two.

vivaoxacafolkart.com> Phil Saviano

FRIENDSHIP BEGINS

Doorbell rang.
White bearded face
A gracious smile stood tall.

Eyes sparkling met an instant of enthrall.
Recognition of inarticulate past,
present connection, future alliance.

Only after years of disclosure
came the truth of soul connection
and verbal recognition.

Windows of the soul
gleam clear without bells or warning
for those who have the gift of sight.

Friendship knows the moment of conception
even if gestation takes a lifetime
for reception.

mmorgenstern

PROSTRATE

Three times stretched out
on pavement before an altar.
A black funereal pall
unfurled over me,
heavy but devoid of warmth.
Six candle stands ensconced,
three on either side, for symbol
not for light.
My body the casket.

My name relinquished.
A sainted patron summoned for protection, emulation.
Joined comrades-in-arms' holy pursuits.

No longer claim to earthly goods
my own body an alien force, resisted.
In exchange
a black wool garment to keep me constrained
and make me sweat unholy smells.

A three-year trial with more or less success—
satisfaction.

A crypt in Rome, cold granite slab my altar
of eternal oblation.
A willing sacrifice as much as could.
Another pall, more funereal candles.
Less comfort than before.

Eternal, perpetual, unfathomable vow
embraced nonetheless.

An anguished urgent plea for acceptance
unanswered in perceptible ways just then
to be touched only in human form
and service.

I accept humanity. I stand upright.
Committed still.

I Stand with Laocoön

Trojan horse—monumental gift—
How could it be refused?
Who can doubt power,
defy authority,
dare to disobey the gods?

Laocoön sensed subterfuge.
Warned his comrades in an adage for the ages:
Beware of Greeks bearing gifts.
Shot an arrow into the wooden belly gorged with deception;
lit a fire at its base.

We are alike, Laocoön, my brother.
Not in marble or plaster,
neither in subterfuge nor violation before an altar.
But in spirit, kin.
Celibate once, but married still.

My fire and spear are words.
I struck the sacred promise false,
warning danger from fabricated fallacious fictions
swathed in lace and flowing frocks
of scarlet, purple, white or black.

Poseidon, Troy's protector, lover of Pelops
and nymph Amphitrite too,
father of Atlas, raped Caeneus,
transformed her into a male warrior.
Who dares defy such fearsome power?

Defiant risk of established power and force
Tests courage to the breaking point.
What fool can stand,
wrestle the demons from the deep
and hope to live, survive, un-mutilated?

I do! cried Laocoön.
I do too, I cried, weeping, shaking.
Knowing we would be punished
for doing wrong,
or for being right.

CAST THE FIRST STONE

Prostitutes prompt in me respect and love.
Scripture taught me well.

Those feelings born not of tawdry-cheap,
crass, careless, sensual or commercial craving.

No, I protest. Some exude a promise of divine,
unbounded, unmerited response to need and longing.

Sense the willingness to give,
like a mother with her suckling cherub.

Comforting arms encircling the afflicted,
healing warmth, compassion

instinctive familiarity,
understanding heart beyond price or reckoning.

Christ saw the loving heart
free of hypocrisy and counted it pure,

pregnant with promise, hope of highest union.
The lingering smell of cigarettes and booze

perfume not unlike the traces of incense
wafting in the sanctuary.

The path to the divine—the realm beyond the body—
is sensuous, not possible without incarnate flesh.

I DANCED WITH THE DEVIL

I danced with evil for a time.
Never quite got rhythm, flow.

Music was enthralling, captivating—
never mastered timing, though.

I tried. What interfered with my success?
Some discordant awkwardness with sin.

Or could it have been the pull of decency
that made my feet so leaden

when my head and heart were giddy willing?

TEARS OVER JERUSALEM

My tears are full to filled.
No more room in heart or mind.

Failure seems complete.
Desire to heal reaps defeat.

No words contain the emptiness,
reflect the darkness or distress of

love denied, defiled, rejected;
mere indifference without reflection.

Does it make a difference?
Love rejected, ignored,

in favor of violence, violence,
yes, violence.

Vilify peace, promote vindictiveness
vie via vicious vindication. Win!

Can evil persist, triumph and trample
fragile kindness, love?

Temporary victories, Pyrrhic, newsworthy
'till tears inundate, cleanse defiled sod.

Tears of blood will seal the bond,
wash the sphere and oceans clean.

Who stand by me will share my blood,
and life will triumph over pain.

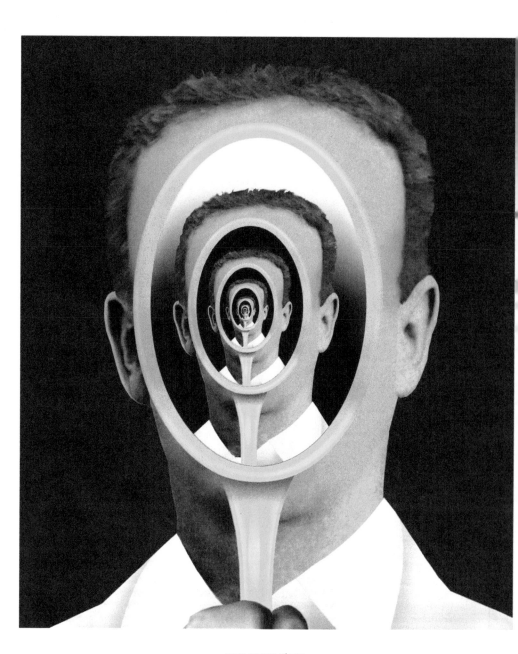

mmorgenstern

SELF KNOWN

Advice, oh Oracle of Delphi,
ancient, deceptive, simple, unadorned.

Know thyself.
Oh, spiritual being striving to be human.

You deal ideal idea
not easy within my grasp.

Honesty, loyalty can be found in youth.
Integrity, self-knowledge takes some time, refinement.

I, the *vigneron* who cultivates and sweats,
presents my soul to the presses

to be mixed and blended.
No man's self is isolated unattended.

A process, not a state you direct,
self-subjected.

Staves pass vintner's tests.
Ooze flavors over many years.

Fermentation is a time-intensive process
Former vintages cure the cask.

Only aging-time can complete the task.
No isolate on mountaintop

has answer for the taste of you.
It is you who drink the product of your years.

INTEGRITY

A noble goal,
fractured path,
beware integrity.

Tears one up inside.
How could it not?
Binding the tattered edges of a soul.

Divided heart
torn apart, desires clashing;
light and darkness fighting for their space.

Past and future vie to take the now.
Surrender takes the prize
to be and not to strive.

Nature has its way.
Harmonize with the universe
if I but take my part.

And willingly
pay the price.

TIME

That precious
ir-repeatable
irredeemable
gift—
Time.

Measured in eons
centuries
years
decades
days, hours.

I can imagine eons,
research centuries
count years
remember decades
record days and hours

but I can only live this instant.
That precious ir-repeatable moment
I have now.
The gift.

mmorgenstern

AT MY GRAVESIDE

Tell no lies
as you give me to my grave.

Fear not my imperfections.
They were cause for good.

My peace with the universe
embraces light and darkness.

Scars speak of battles
won and lost;

my faults served some others well—
all worth the cost.

Truth alone will honor
what I've been or done.

COURAGE: SHOW YOURSELF

I

Come from the shadows
Defy displays.
Rip yourself from glossy
glitzy front-page images,
photo-shopped to shiny
perfection.
Disregard the golden medals,
outstretched victorious arms
fluttering flags behind you.

II

Show yourself as you have to me:
Your matted hair,
Sweat-drenched skin
dust coated into mud.
I trembled at cries of
birth pains
and finally took some blame.
You pierced my ear
with a yelp at the news:
Your son is dead.
Maccabees' anguish matched.

Yes, Courage, you are mother,
my mother, every mother
complex, contradictory.
Life-giving, enduring, fighting.
Makes no matter man or maid.
Force from the heart and loins
of either is the same.

Sighs of daily labor
go unremarked.
Tears over war and conflict

stronger than any armament;
last beyond
racial–any hate.

III

Mother courage melds
into the colors
of the universe;
purple-green majestic mountains,
waves of taupe desert dunes,
azure caressing beaches,
and ravenous white forces
hammer-sculpt rainbow granite
deposit of eons.

Hues of dawn and sunset
each day reflect her power.

She endures.

awrsipe

A CHRISTMAS SERMON

I

Things move, things happen
each year around December.
One hums a carol
sends cards,
chooses gifts,
bakes special.
A glow may come,
delighting,
embarrassing a little.
Christmas spirit,
is it?

Pass it off.
It's all for the children,
cover up.
Recall how the children's eyes light up
at the shiny tree.
Distract yourself.
Anticipate how happy children are going to be
when they get a gift they wanted
but didn't expect
because it was too expensive.
And, of course, it was too expensive.
But that's Christmas
for children.

Preoccupation—
Something's missing?
Sadness—
It hasn't been a good year.
Can't get in the spirit.
Gifts won't be big,
not elaborate,
will the kids understand?

Somehow defend against the sadness.
Thoughts can protect me:
Christmas is for the kids.

II

I can protect myself
against the Christmas spirit.
The Scrooge inside me,
practical grouch
submerged in daily cares,
really too busy to know or care.
Busy.
Dishes, diapers, running noses, bikes,
bruises, pills, bills and payments,
job, boss, promotion, holding on
inside, outside, hurts and slights.

No time,
there is not time.
No time for dreams,
too much to do.
No time for spirit,
we don't have time.
No time for time,
and Christmas is a time.
A time to stop.

I'm practical.
Not comfortable to stop.

This is not really for children.
Fourth of July fireworks light up kids' eyes.
Parties, presents, birthdays, trips
cause children happy anticipation.
This is a time for busy adults to stop.

III

To understand Christmas spirit
one needs to
sin a little
suffer a little
live a little
love a little.
Christmas is for grownups.

Because I'm a sinner I can understand
the spirit of Christmas.
The bitterness of a mistake
gives me an appetite for forgiveness.
The weight of grudges carried
can only be relieved by giving them up,
by forgiving.
Children haven't sinned enough
or long enough
to savor the smell,
the fragrance, the taste
of forgiveness.
And this time is forgiveness.

Suffering? At Christmas?
There is enough—too much:
sickness, separations, conflicts,
disappointments,
tears, sleeplessness, worries. Wars,
silent restless agony and loneliness.
Suffering I let surface only in the
middle of the night.
I can embrace my suffering in the dark time
when the lights on a tree twinkle.
Restlessness makes me reach out
to embrace good will
for comfort,

for peace.
This is the time I long for peace.

This is when I experience the care,
the labor of daily living, and ask
what is it all about?
Who is it for?
I can see hope more clearly.
There is hope in the living, in the smallest,
the least of us.

I have had to love,
at times a little hopelessly, blindly,
to see the spirit of the time.
Experience and disappointment
tunes me to the sound of giving.
Open ears, open heart
open to the sounds of joy
the cries for love,
this spirit, this time.
My hearing to the message of love
not easily won. Not cheap.
Not in blares nor blasts.
I hear the sighs, the whimper,
the silent sounds of love.
A baby born,
a lover....

IV

Some spirit tempts me
more easily this time of year.
When I slow down,
it moves me. It makes me afraid
when I realize
I have lived too long without it.

Christmas is not for children.
It is for busy folks like me
who have to stop
and look at the children.

I see their excitement and wonder,
tears and disappoints.
I look with a certain amount of envy
at innocence and simplicity
for a sordid and selfish world.

The power of a baby born is stunning.
Power to move a tired heart.
Swaddled helplessness
strong enough to inspire
the enemy within,
moving me
to forgive life, abandon resentments
and make peace.
This is power.
Love that confounds,
making sharing seem natural.

No–Christmas is too much for children,
too much to handle.
I have to help children embrace it, treasure it.
When children grow up they will know
the spirit is to be fully alive.

awrsipe

SPEAK JUDAS SPEAK

I
THE PIT

No flicker of warmth.
No hint of momentary relief.
Imminent dissolution?
No alleviation of immanent fear.
Anticipation.
When the flash of fire?
Armageddon or just death?

Swaddled in the stultification
of frost and freezing.
Isolation. Where is consolation
from the tingle of getting shivers-cold?
Deprived even that finger-blue-biting
connection with frostbite.
Frozen reality would be some comfort.

Trapped in this empty pit
filled with void.
Suffocating in nothingness
Choking on purposelessness.
No light, no sound,
no echo even of the emptiness.
The faint smell of tar and feces
wafts one reassuring sensation.

Is this the last exit from reality?
where crucifixion or rape
provide alleviation? Salvation?
Damnation?
Welcome destructive distractions
sultry satisfactions.

Or could this be real?
Reality beyond reality?

An entry to the mysterious realm of the real?
Inaccessible by reason. Experience of heart.

No power, force nor word holds sway.
The coin of this realm is endurance, courage
and radical openness—new existence—
a heart still beating, rent asunder
on a pagan altar by a sacred ritual Tumi
or a trepanation of the soul
now relieved of earthy pressure.

Time or place have no relation to this geography.
Fallen angels fill the place
but take no space
in this spaceless emptiness.
Abstraction has no power,
neither companion nor tormentor.

II
PRESENCE

An unthreatening rustle.
A voice wordlessly shouts
"There is no escape."

I feared this was bottomless,
though I hoped it might be a portal
—new dimension.
Despite the ominous message,
I responded with relief:

Welcome, comrade.
I feared I was alone.
Tell me who you are and
why you share my distress.

*I am Judas and it is you who share
my distress*, he spoke with a tone of consolation.

I have been closer than you know
for a long time now.

It is my assignment
I am man. I am man. I am man.

He wailed with passionate insistence:
My commission is to be with those
torn apart by the spirit of
my friend.
He is the flame. To be close to him
is to burn like the bush-not-destroyed.

I am the poor always with you.
The leper, the blind, the outcast.
I am as close to you as your heart.
I am part of you, my friend.

III
THE CONFESSION

Speak, Judas.
Tell me your story.
Can you tell me how we come to this desolation?
Is this the punishment for my sins?

Judas laughed,
and I responded;
I read of you and your suffering.
Thought I knew your destiny.
Judas laughed.

I told him I felt an affinity with him,
convinced he is misunderstood—
a particular pain I know.

I was counting all my sins.
Expected this and worse,
but hoped time on earth

would count for some reprieve.
Loneliness.
Did love count?

I embraced love, lust, fully as I could.
La petite mort—always a pained reminder
of lonely distance, separation.

Giving me no chance to tell my story
or shrive my conscience,
Judas blurted his confession first.

I am man, he repeated,
as if to remind me, justify himself.
He went on:
Temple prostitutes
guided my early manly stirrings
and filled my loins with life.

The perfume, tresses, softness
of their breasts and arms
intoxicated me.
The thought of their moist lips and loins
still catches me at moments unprepared,
a helpless boy
subject to a body's longing
for garrulous, luscious love and kindness.

He continued:

Some temple harlots, men of beauty,
came to our service to instruct, enjoy.
Dizziness filled my body with
the throbbing of insistence,
confusion and completion
as they ministered with compassion,
ecstasy.

I knew it all.
I knew it all.
Judas said this without
the slightest tone of shame, remorse,
nor any hint of braggadocio.

Graven gods, Baal's temple held no hold on me.

I could see now the tears in his voice.

He told his tale simply,
without elaboration,
leaving me stung,
woefully sore
without relief for my predicament.

Trapped. Still weighted with
unnamed guilt and writhing in this punish pit.

Judas seemed free.
His truth even quelled the horror of our place.

In fact, the walls of the pit
that first posed solid, impenetrable,
suddenly appeared translucent.

We are going to see an exit, Judas said.
I reminded him he said
there was no escape.

He retorted:
There is no escape from love, pain or death.
I did not say there is no exit
from this path of desolation.

My companion continued
as if reading from a ritual:

"Confession heals, justifies,
grants pardon for sins.

This is the chance for mercy.
Believe it. Never despair.
Hope."

IV
THE PATH OF LOVE

My companion continued his confession
as if I were not there.

My lust for life-love led me to Magdalene.
She was the most desirable
of all the women of Jerusalem.
Her charm, gracefulness, graciousness,
exuded an aura of awesomeness that
overwhelmed me.
Nothing could hold me back from
her magnetism that filled my being,
body, spirit, mind and soul.

Her social station left nothing
to be desired. It was a welcome challenge
to my humble beginnings and overweening ambition.
I could prove myself by winning her approval.

Love blossomed
and impregnated me with an
inexhaustible thirst for love.

She became a companion.
My companion.
Her love,
her body,
her being,
was too grand for me;
for any one man alone.

I introduced her to some of my brothers.
John was filled with grand ideas and words,

but he was needy, shy.
His spirit flourished under her care.
His enthusiasm glowed
when he experienced her love, acceptance.
Peter was simply lonely—
as any man can get.

Once the Master became Magdalene's friend
everything changed for all of us.
Love took on a different dimension.

We were transformed as brothers, friends,
closer than any family,
one spiritual organism.

He held our body, spirit, mind, soul.
Sensation fused all into unity.
We had a cause far beyond ourselves.

V
COMMISSION

I had been prepared for the transformation.
He held me in his arms
the night before he shared
—himself—
his Bread and Wine—himself—
Is there any way to name it?

He told me all that I would suffer—
all that I would be:
the outcast, the perpetual human pustule,
pimpled spiritual leper.
The despised betrayer.

I was destined to be man.
I am man, man writ large.
Destined to carry all devils within my heart.

Destined to love full measure,
to live and embrace all of life
as neither saint nor god, but as a simple man.

Humanity his gift and promise.
He shared this precious nature,
the crown of creation.

As he held me close
his breath was warm upon my neck,
my strength transformed within,
beyond any tactile vigor.
I could accept my destiny,
embrace his commission
to be part of his story.

Only those who did not know me
could imagine my demise as self-inflicted.
You will see.

VI
THE KISS

In the garden
he kissed me full on my receptive lips.
No sense of reserve or rejection.
Our love, acceptance, forever misunderstood.
Perpetual rejection
the price of our friendship
still the cornerstone,
part of his plan of life
many still cannot accept.
We are bound together
by an essence of nature
in the spiritual universe
grasping all humankind.

VII
Transformation

Judas said he told me all he could.
He was no betrayer.

The last signs of our confinement
began to disappear.

The walls of the pit became evanescent.
Secure now in a cloud of fog I could not know.

It was also a desert—
Judas' perpetual dwelling.

He spoke his last words to me
as he walked across the open sands.

Like Jacob
we have wrestled with the Angel.

You and I, crippled for life.
We limp for our cause.

We have participated
in the greatest victory a man can have—

the one he wins over himself
and his arrogance.

VIII
THE END

I was not meant to have
the crown of martyrdom.

I was not made to be a saint.
I was destined to tell the truth.
My fortune is
to seize courage,
to be human.

SURVIVOR'S LAMENT / DAILY COURAGE

I

If courage begins in a crib
with tears of loss and separation,
dealing with desolation, trauma, frustration,
its end is problematic.
I have seen the bars turn to iron
and heard cries for milk, now
agony moans for deadly drugs,
pills and potions,
prescriptions forged or stolen.

Seen lithe young limbs
pock-marked with traces of infected needles.
Been at bedsides,
death too young, too young, too young.
Funerals without mourners,
bodies just abandoned,
all friends gone.
Alone, alone, alone
without the protection of the bars.

Not that these tortured, afflicted
brothers and sisters are different
from me;
their traumas were distinct,
more horrible, more devastating, debilitating.
Luck, blessings, not on their side
when betrayal ripped their life to shreds,
tore apart their soul
irreparably, irreparably, irreparably.

II

When caught,
even when suspected,
the perpetrator, sponsor, institution

blamed the victim. "They were vulnerable."
Aren't we all? "See their crimes, their sins."
What flaws in us made us easy prey?
Valid victims? Repositories for your guilt.
How can you justify your image-self-serving?
At our expense, our expense, our sacrifice?

You are powerful, I concede.
Your officer says, "If you talk, we will crush you."
The bishop says, "I only lie when I have to." Or
"street-wise kids are seducing naïve priests."
Many of us have felt the sting of your power,
the force of your resistance, lies.
Let others judge facts, render opinions.
I will stand by what I can't deny,
the testimony of experience, my wounds and others'.

No grand gesture nor dramatic scene
will advance the cause from me.
Daily effort, struggle. That's what I revere.
I sit and witness tears, black, blood-red, bile-green
and crystal-clear wrenching stories too sordid for the press.
I've gone to meetings, heard sobering accounts
of trauma by torture and neglect.
I've seen it: shame oozing from pores of hearts ripped apart,
souls tattered, guilt misplaced, undeserved, wrenching guts.

III

I cry. I wail, even shriek at night—at three A.M.
when none but darkness is to hear me weep.
Betrayal real—re-imagined, re-lived—not fantasy.
Do you understand?
So many don't.
Power rules. Power crushes. Power seems triumphant.
Fear can overtake me, fill empty soul with bleak remorse,
"What could have been?" For me? For you?
Can't let darkness conquer. Hang on until pink light.

Hang on, hang on, hang on, if that is all I do.
I rouse my spirit from my crib.
I penetrate whatever bars that bind,
stand and cry, "Freedom. I can be free.
Your courage, daily, makes it so."
Hope rings in your honesty.
I summon courage, rage for integrity
from your spirit whistling through that
heart-hole made whole,
my Aeolian harp.

Your courage gives me courage, and your words.
They are my sword and shield now.
Your friendship guides me from the field of strife.
Battered by our quest and cause,
but I have survived.

No crowns, no flags, will mark the victory.
The day, well lived, reward enough.
Your gift to me, the courage of endurance,
flows in my veins
I gratefully pass it on at Three A.M.

ACKNOWLEDGEMENTS

Donald Winnicott, British pediatrician and psychoanalyst, was most sensitive to child development and especially how early neglect and trauma affects adult life and relationships. He also contributed to an understanding of how intervention—a therapeutic safe place "holding relationship"—could help a child grow and translate his or her deficits into strengths. These outpourings benefit from reflections on these issues.

Experience has made me profoundly indebted to Winnicott's ideas. Great good fortune has given me inspiration and holding relationships that have been sustaining and vital. We are bound together by the *cause* that I laud in *The Warrior's Lament*.

It has been a privilege to know Vincent Felitti, prime mover of the Adverse Childhood Experiences (ACE) Study, a most powerful tool to understand and intervene in the long-term consequences of early abuse and neglect.

I have no better word than *friend* —in its fullest resonance—to credit the sustenance and inspiration of the group that has given me living models and meaning since 1990. Tom Doyle, my real pastor; Jeff Anderson, an unequaled mentor; Sylvia Demarest, John Manly and Patrick Wall, dedicated lawyers I was honored to work with; Michael D'Antonio and Michael Rezendes, Pulitzer-Prize-winning journalists who encouraged me in my faltering word excursions; Marianne Benkert, my companion every step of the way and our son, Walter, a psychiatrist who has lent even his forensic courage to the cause.

Terry McKiernan, faithful friend, has frequently left his duties in Boston to support my work and spirits. He is founding director of BishopAccountability.org . He and Anne Barrett Doyle, co-director, tirelessly gather and catalogue the facts about sexual abuse, primarily in the RC Church, but have formed a database that helps combat all abuse across the world. Friend Phil Saviano, an agitator of the best sort, lit the fuse in Boston that moved us all to action. Bill Kenney has been a technical advisor and emergency resource that pulled this manuscript out of the dumpster many times. Pearl Yu is a medical advisor who pulled me out of some tight places. Robin Hatcher is a writer-analyst friend of many years. I am indebted to them—life-givers all.

Marianne assembled a "household staff"—Sherry Perez, Mike Law, Alecia Ryden, Anne Hassidim and some weekly visitors who are like family. Emma Pickering of Friesen Press solved crucial problems that brought my written efforts to completion. These are the people who have literally kept me alive, and more, included me in the *cause*, inspired me, gave me reasons to live, work and love.

The bond is not temporal. The cause of protecting children and preventing abuse will continue. These people are fighting the good fight. Their courage is powerful and their impact wide-ranging and an influence for good.

Words fail to express my admiration and gratitude adequately for my friends.

Some things are inexpressible.

AWRS Easter 2017

NOTES

Michael Morgenstern is an award-winning artist and illustrator whose work has graced the covers and pages of a wide range of magazines and publications from *The Economist* to *The New York Times*. His work has inspired me for years. His design for the cover and most of the pieces in these pages are meant to provoke reflection. His life is a testimony to the power of art and healing. His art inspires my mind, heart and words. His life is courageous beyond reckoning.

Michael D'Antonio is a Pulitzer-Prize-winning investigative journalist who can be seen often on CNN TV. He is a smart, vigorous and generous gentleman from New England. A prolific writer, among his recent books are *The Truth About Trump*; *Mortal Sins: Sex, Crime, and the Era of Catholic Scandal*; and most recently, *A Consequential President: The Legacy of Barack Obama*.

Michael Rezendes won a Pulitzer Prize along with the Spotlight Team of the Boston Globe for exposing the cover-up of sexual abuse in the Catholic Church; they recorded the process of that historic journalistic investigation in *Betrayal*, which formed part of the impetus for the 2016 Academy-Award-winning movie *Spotlight* where he is aptly portrayed by Mark Ruffalo. He has a spark that ignites those lucky enough to be around him.

Terry McKiernan is the founding president of *BishopAccountability.org*, which since 2002 has been a resource and database dedicated to consolidating and preserving records of the RC clergy sexual abuse crisis. The service collects and makes available the largest known deposit of published documents about individual Catholic and institutional violations of minors and vulnerable adults. He is a scholar of the first order.

ABOUT THE AUTHOR

A.W. Richard Sipe began writing poetry after his 80th birthday. Unintentionally, that production, entitled I Confess, turned out to be the beginning of a memoir that reflected his concurrent work in psychoanalysis. Courage is the continuation of his earlier process. It reflects his deep commitment to the years of struggle with the sexual problems of the Catholic Church, specifically advocating for those abused by bishops and priests.

Photo by Nel Cepeda, for the *San Diego Union Tribune.*

Sipe began his career spending 18 years as a Benedictine monk and priest. His earliest interest was in the interface between spirituality and psychology / religion and psychiatry. In that capacity, he was trained to deal with the mental health concerns of clergy. He has published eleven books on his interests and experience. These studies and research, with some guidance from Margaret Mead, led to the landmark publication in 1990 of *A Secret World: Sexuality and the Search for Celibacy* and the 1996 *Sex, Priests, and Power: The Anatomy of a Crisis.* The latter was one instrument used in the 2002 Boston Globe Pulitzer Prize-winning Spotlight investigation of clergy abuse and recorded in the 2016 Best Movie Academy Award given to the movie Spotlight.

Richard practiced therapy for 28-years in Baltimore; his career also involved teaching on every level of education from grade school to graduate school. He has been an associate professor of psychology in Catholic universities, major seminaries and for twenty-five-years part time lecturer on family therapy at Johns Hopkins University Department of Psychiatry and Behavioral Sciences. Since 1988 he has acted as an expert witness and consultant in civil and criminal cases that involve sexual abuse of the vulnerable, mainly by clergy.

All of Sipe's experiences and struggles are reflected in the pathos and promise of his poetic outpourings. His gratitude to his friends is a major factor in his ability to continue his work and scholarship. His wife of 47 years, Marianne Benkert, a psychiatrist, and their son Walter, also a psychiatrist, have shared some of the same interests and commitments. He and his wife are now retired in La Jolla, California.

Who among us is ready to face death with eyes and heart completely open? Who among us is ready to account for all that we have said and done, for all our battles lost and won? Who among would have the courage to pause at the very fulcrum of life and death and carefully consider whether it is time to lay down one's shield and fall upon one's sword, or pray for "Galahad's strength of ten" and fight again?

In these poems of hope, reflection and spirituality, Richard Sipe endures a dark night of the soul and lingers there, daring darkness to overwhelm him and spare him yet another battle, while trying to believe in one more dawn. "What fool can stand, wrestle the demons from the deep, and hope to live, survive, un-mutilated?" he complains.

But the answer is Sipe himself, as he recalls the dream childhood, a dance with the devil and a path to the divine through sensuality and the ceaseless tests of maturity. Summoning the courage to stand at his own graveside, he reviews his scars, his imperfections and his faults with uncommon candor, concluding, "Truth alone will honor what I've been or done."

—Michael Rezendes,
Pulitzer-Prize-Winning Investigative Writer, *The Boston Globe*

A.W. Richard Sipe—mentor and champion for victims of clergy sexual abuse—records here, as he did in his prior volume *I Confess,* his wrestling with personal demons and angels, ones that occur behind the veil of the man we all see.

Courage at Three AM says, simply, I am human, a man. I have lived life's paradoxes, its arrows of broken integrity and its abuses of soul and meaning which, over time, demand a hearing by haunting the 3AMs of our waking dreams. Like Judas we all face the challenge of transformation, resolution and reintegration of our paradoxical parts.

The courage needed to dance with the 3AM muses, is the same required for the realization and acceptance that we need someone to tell us "one more time" that we are loved and were born to be loved…. not abused, forgotten or caste aside.

Courage at Three AM teaches us that our scars of inner conflict are not to be feared, covered up, lied about or air-brushed away. Rather, our collective and individual scars need to be embraced because they are our own essential life-marks that identify who we are, collectively and individually.

—Stephen de Weger,
Queensland University of Technology, Brisbane | Australia

In his new book of poems, *Courage at Three AM*, Richard Sipe continues the reckoning he began in *I Confess* – but with a difference. These new poems are more personal and unguarded, closer to the bone. Sipe grapples with the discouragement and the terror of old age, and the weariness that comes from fighting a powerful institution. He began his work on the inside, as a therapist helping his fellow priests. But over the years, his scholarship on celibacy and his advocacy for the survivors of clergy abuse brought him more and more into conflict with the church that had been his spiritual home. In a remarkable long poem in the new collection, reminiscent of James Merrill's Ouija-board books, Sipe imagines an encounter with Judas that ultimately resolves that conflict – he feels an affinity for the man another poet has called "Saint Judas."

Ultimately Sipe finds a solution to the despair of old disagreements and old age in the youthful sources of his commitment – a beautiful poem evokes his vivid boyhood memory of a Minnesota morning. Other poems imagine his experience back to infancy, the core of Catholic imagery. And in a poem about death, Sipe parses all the time of his life down to the present infinitesimal moment, a happy counterpart to the anguished, early morning moment of the book's title. These poems are by turns mystical and practical – in the end, Sipe takes simple comfort in the example of abuse survivors and in his friends. This is a book about time, and its most enduring image is of a first visit with a friend, the "instant of enthrall" when the "years of disclosure" began.

—Terence McKiernan, President
BishopAccountability.org

I Confess: courageous, funny, provocative, raw, delightful. **Catholics finally have a Philip Roth!** Some of it, too, is downright searing, the Catholic reality that I am glad is, in this elegantly subjective way, preserved.

—Tom Roberts / Editor at large /National Catholic Reporter

Available at AMAZON.com and FRIESENPRESS.com

I CONFESS

HOW A VERY RELIGIOUS CATHOLIC BOY
LEARNED DIRTY WORDS SEX and CELIBACY
AVOIDED SUICIDE EMBRACED DEATH
FOUND LOVE GOD & HIMSELF
NOT NECESSARILY IN THAT ORDER
A. W. Richard Sipe

G&MGildin 1991

CPSIA information can be obtained
at www.ICGtesting.com
Printed in the USA
LVOW05*2123220917
549749LV00011B/62/P